THE GREAT DIVIDE–VISITED

CLAIMING GOD'S GRACE

The Great Divide–Visited
by Catherine Bergstrom

Printed in the United States of America

ISBN 1-59781-439-3

Photo of author: Philip Kent, Tysons Corner, Virginia.

www.xulonpress.com

This book is dedicated to all those who are wondering and searching for God in their everyday lives.

Table of Contents

An Acknowledgment With Thanks to Gail Mathews

When I needed help transforming my handwritten stories into the electronic age, "someone who knew someone" put Gail and I in touch. That is how casually our working relationship began over four years ago, and we've never actually met face to face; we even live in different states.

We connect through the postal service or by phone, but Gail's great patience and understanding of my purpose have really connected us—now through two manuscripts. I learned right away how capable she is and came to appreciate her encouragement and gentle spirit.

Whenever I had doubts about putting my writing into print, I thought about the support God had sent to me—especially through you, Gail—and I continued. Thank you.

Preface

Perhaps the best way to write a preface for this book is to begin with a question for you, the reader.

If you believed God's promise that He wouldn't give you more than you could bear, how do you think God would hold you up when the unbearable happened? How do you think He would comfort you?

Maybe you haven't thought about that. I certainly had not. I just told myself that the loss of one of my children would be so unbearable that God wouldn't be able to help me, so therefore, I thought—with a little shudder in my soul—He would never let me suffer such a loss. (God had seemed somewhat remote to me, but I believed His promises.) That is all I allowed myself to think . . . until we lost our beloved son, David, when his Navy jet crashed (see Appendix), and in total devastation I called on God's promise to comfort, to help me—in my inconsolable grief—to bear the unbearable.

How did I think He would do that? I didn't ask. I just knew. I realize now how God's grace was present at that moment.

He gave me absolute trust in Him.

His gifts of comfort were extraordinary, and months later I even felt compelled to write a book about that, *I Know This is What I'm Supposed to Do: A Story of Loss and Comfort.*

As the months and now years have passed since we lost

David, I continued to receive and cherish God's grace and the Holy Spirit. It raised a question, though, of how and why for most of my life I had failed to "have ears to hear and eyes to see" God's grace.

The question grew deeper. I began to use the phrase "the Great Divide" to describe that place that existed in my mind.

Occasionally I gave a brief talk in church, and I kept writing stories. I began to understand that the answer to my question was in my writing. I had always been receiving God's grace, and some of those moments of grace were now being brought to my memory, but I just hadn't acknowledged or accepted them at the time.

So this is my book of stories—personal—all written in the last three years, even though some reach far back in my life. Maybe you, too, will catch glimpses of that Divine Power who surrounds us all . . . if we will just accept Him.

CHAPTER I

KNOWING AND NOT KNOWING—
BUT REMEMBERING

But the Helper, the Holy Spirit, whom the Father will send in My name, He will teach you all things, and bring to your remembrance all that I said to you. John 14:26

January-February 2001

I have a question.
    It gnaws away at me
but I don't know what the question is.
    I believe the Holy Spirit
comforted me in extraordinary ways.
    Some ways I can't find even
the words to describe.
    But they are there
and I've been compelled
    to write them anyway.
Those I could.
    But what is their meaning anyway?
Am I a soul to be pitied?
    A soul to be patronized by the church?
What would the church say about
    the Gifts of Comfort I received?
I've never heard this discussed in church.
    Or did I and I didn't understand?
One thing I always believed, understood:
    God would not give me more
than I could bear. He promised.
    Then the unbearable happened.
We lost our beloved son.
    God promised.
    What is my question?

“Set-up” in the Great Divide

Being justified as a gift by His grace through the redemption which is in Christ Jesus. Romans 3:24

I would say, in retrospect, that the Great Divide was living in God’s grace and knowing it, and living in God’s grace and not knowing it.

I’ve always called myself a Christian ever since I can remember, but I lived a divided life. My spiritual life, my faith, was focused on a God who was rather remote, who lived somewhere else . . . heaven? I, meanwhile, lived here on Earth, and the two were connected only by prayer, as needed. The divide between secular and spiritual wasn’t close to 50/50; it was more like 90/10. By that I mean that 90 percent of the time I was out there fending for myself (and I didn’t think I was doing too bad of a job), and 10 percent of the time I called on Him for help.

When I was younger, I remember hearing that slang expression “They got religion.” It was used, not necessarily derisively, to explain a religious awakening in another person, and it was the reason that perhaps you didn’t see that person anymore. I wondered why folks who “got religion” seemed to disappear, and I felt a little sadness. What was wrong with the secular world? After all, God created it. Wasn’t I a Christian? I didn’t want to go into seclusion.

So if you'll forgive my use of another slang expression, I was "set up": I had unknowingly set myself up for a new way of thinking, for a new way of understanding—through suffering.

Suffering

Blessed are those who mourn, for they shall be comforted.
Matthew 5:4

Many of the Christian writers say that, for some, only in a time of great personal suffering do we start to develop a relationship with God. Only then do we drop our facade of self-sufficiency; only then do we recognize that we aren't in control; only then are we closest to accepting God's will in our lives. That is certainly true for me.

I know that God doesn't engineer suffering and tragedy in our lives just so He can reach us. But He knows what life will inevitably bring and He is there in our suffering and pain if we call on Him. But that raised a big question for me. "Where have I been all my life?" How had I managed to go through the routine of being a Christian—attending church, seeing that my children were raised in the church, even daily prayer—and missed out on the living Bible, the presence of the Holy Spirit, and a personal relationship with our Savior. I thought that personal relationship was only attainable by putting oneself in a kind of religious trance. Really.

Does God give us eyes that don't see and ears that don't hear? The Bible makes reference to that (Isaiah 6:9-10). He never demands we do something. There is always that choice He gives us.

Choosing

Come Unto Me. Matthew 11:28

I'm a little fearful, closing that Great Divide. It takes absolute trust that God will continue a good work begun in me. I'm not in control and I flounder with tears and doubt.

But the gifts of comfort I have received are extraordinary. What is amazing is that, upon reflection, there is a pattern of grace that has flowed through my life. I just never stopped and grabbed hold to learn and receive those gifts of the Holy Spirit. It is actually painful to think of what I have missed.

So here I am. I "got religion" but I live in a secular world and I'm bombarded with a secular culture that says it is supreme. So should I seek isolation? Disappear into an environment that doesn't question, that always nurtures? Reverse the divide, so to speak—10/90 instead of 90/10? No!

"Whether therefore ye eat or drink, or whatever ye do, do all to the Glory of God." I Corinthians 10:30.

That Bible verse heads up Chapter 10, "The Sacrament of Living," in A. W. Tozer's book *The Pursuit of God.* The chapter was like a light coming on for me. Tozer starts out the chapter by writing, "One of the greatest hindrances to internal peace which the Christian encounters is the common habit of dividing our lives into two areas—the sacred (spiritual) and the secular (natural)." [p. 117]

Wow! What a relief. I'm not the only one who struggles with the Great Divide! What a challenge . . . no, God didn't give this as a challenge. The truth is in front of me to accept, and then by prayer and trust to live it, that "sacramental quality of everyday living" whereby the secular and sacred are not in opposition. All that I am as a human is what God created. Why, then, do I see tears and longing as secular? Because they don't glorify God? True. As the Apostle Paul might say (when he had seemingly contradictory understandings), "What then?" And I could say, "Our Lord Jesus wept." Yes, God understands our memories and tears and doubts and accepts them (maybe even as sacred?). But He would have me grow through it—by His grace, to His glory. I pray.

Furthermore, I am a witness, not by reason of credentials or status or knowledge but, like countless numbers of you, through our personal experiences—gifts given by the Holy Spirit. His gifts that must be claimed as our own because the Great Divide, after all, was a place of my own making.

So I go forward, knowing on the one hand that God is present and wondering at other times where He is. I live life as an ordinary person in the presence of extraordinary love . . . always accepting His grace.

Hebrews 2:1. *For this reason we must pay much closer attention to what we have heard, lest we drift away from it.*

May 13, 2003

Confirmation Class

When asked to share my story of faith with the confirmation class at our church, I prepared this brief synopsis of my journey. I place it near the beginning of my book of stories, as it helps to tie them together in time and location.

Good afternoon:

It is a privilege to be here with your confirmation class. You are receiving a discipline in faith—a discipline that unlocks doors; that gives you tools with which to communicate; that provides you with pastors and mentors you can talk with and question. You lucky kids!

I have a story to tell you—a confirmation story in reverse, you might say.

The story begins in a little town in Montana (population 1,800) in the 1940s, a wonderful place to be as a kid. There certainly wasn't television or mega-movie theaters or computer games, but there was ice skating on the frozen river in the winter, hiking in the hills, fishing, hunting rattlesnakes on a hot summer day, all-day family picnics in the mountains on Sundays, and the confidence of knowing everyone in town.

There were also the usual dangers, and the person about

whom this story is told encountered a few. She was hit in the head at age four by exploding bullet fragments (some of the older kids threw bullets into a bonfire to see what would happen); she smashed into a moving truck at age eight while riding her bike downtown; and there were various other misfortunes.

Eventually, they moved to a larger city in Montana when she was ten. And again they moved to Minnesota when she was fifteen. Her new friends in Minnesota were good kids, and they enjoyed movies, skating, dancing, and swimming, and gave their parents no reason to worry. She was going to be a senior in high school (where this story picks up) but was only sixteen, and some of the boys in her group of friends were already attending the university.

One warm summer evening they were invited to attend a party at the lake home of a friend of one of her group and they decided to go. They got there early, most of the guests weren't there yet, and the host, Mac, asked the teenager how she and "Rocky," his friend, were getting along. They talked and walked along the lake shore, finally ending up standing on a dock at another lake-front property. Inexplicably, Mac said he was going swimming and dived off the dock. Time passed. When he didn't reappear, the teenager began calling out to him, "Mac, don't tease me, please tell me where you are." She thought he might be hiding under the dock or had swum far out on the lake. It was getting dark and she was in a totally unfamiliar place. But Mac didn't reappear. She said in a more frantic voice, "If you don't come up, I'm going to call for help." He didn't reappear. She began screaming for help and people came running.

Her friend Rocky was a trained lifeguard and he immediately jumped into the water, only to find Mac at the bottom of the lake at the end of the dock. They tried to revive him but couldn't. Emergency vehicles came and desperate minutes passed. Finally her friends led her back to the car to take her home, but as they walked past the many residents of the lake cabins, who had come out in response to all the commotion, she heard one woman's voice saying, "She probably pushed him in."

Now she felt desperately alone—a young man whom she'd just met was dead, she was the only witness (and now, she thought, viewed with suspicion), she was at a party she shouldn't have been at in the first place, her mother would not understand, and after she got home the police came to question her.

Where had everything gone wrong? Who would understand? Who would know what was in her heart and what had actually happened . . . and why?

This sixteen-year-old's early exposure to Christianity had been neighbors who, for a few years, had taken her to their church for Sunday School. Her own parents never talked about God and didn't belong to a church until she was in high school.

But God's grace is extraordinary, and so the sixteen-year-old knew where to go, knew who would know what had happened. So she prayed, "God, you know what is in my heart. You know what happened and that is all that matters to me." Then she rested in that prayer.

The investigation into the accident showed that the cause was diving into an unfamiliar body of water without knowing the depth there or about any possible obstruction in the water . . . there was a huge boulder at the end of the dock and Mac had hit his head. The teenager's good friends made sure that she got to meet the official in charge of the accident investigation so he could explain all of this to her, so she would know that everyone knew the truth.

The teenager also now knew with certainty that God was her helper and advocate, but she didn't understand much more than that. And she didn't tell anyone about her prayer, because how do you explain the unexplainable? Besides, she didn't know anyone who talked about God. However, she wanted to be closer to that source, that helper and advocate, so she began helping in Sunday School with the kindergarten class. And the summer she graduated from high school she had volunteered through her church for a mission project at a "community center" in St. Louis, Missouri. She had no idea what to expect, but before going to St. Louis, all the young people from across the country who were going on these various missions met in Pennsylvania for a few days of training. She absolutely felt out of place there, as all these young people seemed to know everything—how to pray (even long prayers), the songs to sing, and they knew their Bibles very well. She felt totally inadequate.

But on to St. Louis, where all that was expected of her was to help with the children who came to the "community center," located in a desperately poor, isolated section of St. Louis— segregated children, black children who in the oppressive St. Louis summer heat could not even swim in the public swimming pools because they were children of color. She was stunned by what she saw of poverty and oppression, that the only place blacks and whites could eat together in a restaurant was the local YMCA. No other restaurant allowed black people to eat there with white people.

She learned about herself. She had always been given hand-me-down clothes, nice clothes but not new or her choice. One day on the playground a little girl came up to her and with great deference asked if she could touch the teenager's cotton skirt . . . a hand-me-down! The little girl delicately felt the material between her fingers and then said, "It's so beautiful." That moment would remain forever etched in the teenager's mind. How could she ever again complain about her clothes or what she had?

The summer ended and the teenager began attending the university. She loved it—the excitement of learning, new friends, football and hockey games, and she also had an evening job on campus at the radio and TV station. But she made no attempt to learn more about God. He was her own private source, there whenever she needed to call on Him.

She was a successful student at the university, she graduated, married a fine man she had met while there, and began raising a family. She had two daughters and she did all the things she wanted to do. But following the crisis of a major illness in her life and God's response to her great fear related to that, she also learned that God was her trusted advisor.

Then a son was born, and as her children grew, the mother realized they knew more about God than she did. The girls had been confirmed in the Oslo American Church in Norway and the son right here at Lord of Life twenty years ago this month. Her children talked about God and expressed their belief and faith, something she had not done.

She just didn't know how to express what her heart and soul told her, what her experiences with God had taught her. There had also been a few times when she hadn't taken her concerns to God and those were dreadful times. She hadn't really learned to trust.

So she listened to her children and talked with them and asked them questions, even as they graduated from high school and then college—first the girls and then the son, who wanted to go to the Naval Academy. He was a fine young man, strong in his faith, and his goal after graduating from the Academy was to fly in the F-14 Tomcat, a jet made famous in the *Top Gun* movie. He achieved that goal in spite of eye problems that limited his choice to the back seat, in charge of radar and weapons. He was good at what he did, and after a few years he requested consideration as one of the aviators who fly in air shows around the country. Only four aviators were selected, and he was one. But at an air show in Pennsylvania on Father's Day 2000, his plane crashed and he was killed.

The entire family was distraught beyond belief. The mother now knew devastation and pain as she had never known. She knew there was nothing on earth that would console her. How could she move forward, keep going? Life and its meaning had forever changed.

But God had not. She knew about His promises, that He would not give us more than we could bear. That He would comfort those who mourn.

She called on His promises—in fact, she insisted something like kids sometimes do to their parents . . . "But you promised!" Of course, parents can't always keep their promises, but God can and does. And, of course, she had no idea how He would keep those promises, but knew He would. In the following days, weeks, months, He comforted the mother in extraordinary ways—but He didn't stop there. He told her she had to write it all down. He told her to start reading and studying His word and to tell about the loving, powerful God who is ever present in our lives whether we acknowledge Him or not. The understanding came to her of God's total presence in her life. He was the one in whom she had to have absolute trust.

Here was her confirmation.

As you probably know by now, I am the teenager, the mother in the story, and I pray that you too know God as your present Helper, Advocate, Advisor, and One in whom you place your complete trust.

CHAPTER II

THAT GRACE!

For by Grace you have been saved through faith;
and that not of yourselves, it is the gift of God.
Ephesians 2:8

Resurrection

On the Friday after David's accident, our family drove down to Virginia Beach, Virginia, for a memorial service for David, to be held at the Oceana Base Chapel. There were two chaplains who presided over the service; David's friends gave eulogies; there were beautiful flowers, pictures of David, music, even a bagpiper. There were memorial gifts of all kinds, a missing man formation fly-over right above the street outside the chapel to which we had adjourned after the service, and then a lovely reception at the officer's club. But above all, one moment remains etched in my mind: at the beginning of the service, the senior chaplain read from the eleventh chapter of John, verses 25-26:

Jesus said to her, "I am the resurrection and the life; he who believes in Me shall live even if he dies, and everyone who lives and believes in me shall never die. Do you believe this?"

How often had I heard those verses from John. How often had they seemed like passing words. But the chaplain read them firmly and deliberately, and paused after he read, "Do you believe this?"

The words were for everyone, but the question seemed directed at me. Indeed it was. It is so vivid in my mind. The question was personal—it was a question of my spiritual life or death, though at that moment I didn't understand that. I just remembered it. ". . . and everyone who lives and believes in Me shall never die. Do you believe this?"

And His question hung in the air. He did not say

Can you believe this? or

Will you believe this? or

You do believe this, don't you? or

Why don't you believe this? or

If you believe this, why do you grieve? or

I have told you this; why do you question?

No, His question was direct, requiring a "yes" or a "no" . . . a simple, direct answer, not a

Maybe, or

I'll think about it, or

If I see him again, I will, or

Why? or

How can that be? or

When? [does that happen?] or

Where will we go?

John 11:27. She said to Him, "Yes Lord; I have believed that You are the Christ, the Son of God, even He who comes into the world."

January 2001

My Arrogant Faith

I didn't know it at the time before David's accident, but I think there was a certain arrogance about my faith, almost like a talisman I wore around my neck. I hate to say that, but in light of my overwhelming loss and the incredible experiences afterwards, it looks that way to me. I see that my understanding is so shallow.

It was so easy to "talk" in the abstract about faith issues, to "feel" empathy for others in illness or loss, to "pray" for certain things that I wanted—like more faith and understanding. I was often glib in what I expressed of my knowledge of Christianity.

Oh Lord, I ask for forgiveness.

It was months after David's accident before I began to grasp what I had experienced in total. I had never felt such intense grief; the pain was unbearable. But I realized I was held up, supported, surrounded by a presence so strong (and yet with almost a sweetness) that I am astounded.

My very soul was wrenched from me and then ever so gently, but persuasively, put back in place. There is a certain sweetness that is out there, a peace. Can I reach it? Can I keep it? Am I strong enough? Or weak enough?

Thank You for the gifts of comfort.

Your Grace is sufficient for the day.

Bliss

I remember the evening so well. It was late, but the pain of sorrow was lodged in my stomach and ached so that it seemed impossible to recover. I stopped on my way to bed at the doorway to what had been David's room and looked in at his picture hanging on the wall. Through the tears the reminder came to say my prayers, and God would provide comfort and strength as He had ever since we lost David.

So that evening, just as I reminded myself to pray and was looking into David's room, a light appeared in the corner next to his picture. I was suddenly wrapped in a sense of comfort, well-being, almost joy! It was so extraordinary and wonderful and I just stood there basking in the moment, but then the thought came—"How can this be? How in the midst of grief can I experience this?" I even felt guilty that I would be so comforted while others were suffering. How could I understand this? I had to know and I had to tell someone. The following day, I asked to speak with one of the pastors and described what had happened. Was there really a light? What word could describe such a spiritual moment? Our contemporary use of the word "joy" didn't seem appropriate. Certainly not happiness. Comfort wasn't strong enough. What word? The peace that passes all understanding?

Pastor Jansen said the word was "bliss." Strange—I didn't think of that word often. It is kind of an "over-the-top" word in my thinking—the look on the face of a contented, sleeping baby . . . or the parents when the baby goes to sleep. Bliss, huh?

When I got home I decided to look up the word "bliss" in the dictionary. I've often noticed that there are subtle meanings to words I use, words that I think I understand, but not really. Sure enough, bliss was one of those. The second definition in the dictionary is "spiritual joy!"

Wow! How I would love to know that bliss all the time—how does one hang onto that? I guess it is what some writers would call a "mountaintop experience," but we can't live up there on the mountaintop.

As I look back on this extraordinary experience, this moment of grace, I wonder about my initial reaction—I just marveled at what I had been given and accepted it. Then I wanted so badly to share it, but it was so personal. What could it mean to anyone else?

Maybe that is why I have to write it down—plain words on plain paper—to describe the indescribable . . . to remind myself to trust . . . to know that God's grace is always there. I am a witness.

March 12, 2002

The Rocking Chair

It wasn't really supposed to be in our house, this rocking chair. Not because of the style of it or the dated fabric, but it was David's, the one thing David wanted from my mother's house after she died. This chair had been my dad's, who had died fifteen years earlier, and David said it reminded him of Grandpa because that's where he used to sit and read.

None of the other ten grandchildren had asked for much when my mother died—an old hammock that was always in the yard on Cecelia Place in St. Paul, Minnesota, a candy dish, a croquet set, a trunk, some pictures. But whatever anyone wanted, we shipped it to them, the memories worth a hundred times the actual value of anything. Thus, this rocking chair was in David's Virginia Beach condo and is now in our house, in David's old room, still with the dated fabric, but a comfortable place to sit and read and remember.

So one day I went into David's room for something, and the grief overwhelmed me . . . again. I sat down on the edge of the rocking chair and, without thinking, lamented, "God, you gave us this wonderful son. Why did you take him from us?"

The words were barely out of my mouth when I realized what I had said—to Whom I was asking the question! Then, for the first time in my life, I felt the terrible agony, pain, and despair of Jesus on the cross. My personal grief turned to anguish and remorse at what I had always failed to grasp. And now I wept for that, for all of us.

Do this in remembrance of Me.

CHAPTER III

STRIVING TO KNOW

Cease striving and know that I am God.
Psalm 46:10

March 2002

The Question Not Asked

I have never been reluctant to ask a question; I probably ask too many questions. There have been times when, upon reflection, I've been embarrassed by what I've asked. If possible, I want to know the why, the how, and the where, and I'm not patient. There was an aggressive nature in my questioning.

So after David's accident, I became puzzled at the question I had not asked of David: Why did he always tell me that "I know what I'm doing is dangerous, but I know it is what I'm supposed to do?" He had even told me once that "It could kill me, but I know this is what I'm supposed to do."

What?! How did he know this?

Why? Why keep doing something so dangerous? It was not typical of my nature to ignore his provocative statements, not discuss them with him, but I didn't.

A year and a half after David's accident, the question not asked came down on me with full force. I knew I would never have the answer: David was gone. It was a late December day. Patty, Mark, and the kids had left and I was picking up, straightening up around the house.

Why, why, why hadn't I ever followed up on David's statement with a question? Quite suddenly the overwhelming thought came to me to read the Bible. So I put aside the toys I was picking up, took the Bible from the book shelf, went to the dining room table, sat down, and thought, "Where am I going to start? I don't even know what to look for." I opened the Bible at random and started reading at that place in the New Testament. It was in Luke, chapter 9, verse 44, that Jesus said, "Let these words sink into your ears: The Son of Man is going to be delivered into the hands of men."

Chapter 9:45 goes on: But they did not understand this statement, and it was concealed from them, so that they might not perceive it; and they were afraid to ask Him about this statement.

Now, I do not elevate either David or myself to the level of Jesus or the disciples. But I have come to understand that the Bible "speaks to us" of ourselves, our frailties, our fears, our weaknesses. And perhaps, like the disciples, I did not want to think the unthinkable. I did not want to understand the statement. I could not ask the question.

March 20, 2002

Out of Code

The task seemed straightforward enough—go buy a new clothes dryer. Our old Sears dryer was in danger of erupting with noise and vibration, and since it was twenty-five years old, it seemed prudent to buy a new one. The word prudent here seems ironic with hindsight.

I ran other errands and finally ended up at the Sears store in the appliance department, armed with a sales flyer that Jim and I had studied carefully. I knew what I wanted and the sales price. I was immediately approached by a sales clerk and the conversation went like this:

Clerk: May I help you?

Me: Yes, I need to replace my dryer. It's twenty-five years old and sounds terrible.

Clerk: I should think so [she said without a smile]. The life of a dryer is nine years on average.

Me: Well, I was looking at this one you have advertised for $299.

Clerk: You don't want that one. It doesn't have a range of heating cycles and the consumer guides say that is the most important thing to look for in a dryer. You would be better off buying this dryer over here [we walked around the aisle] that costs $399, but if you buy anything over $399, delivery is free. Since delivery is normally $40, you end up paying only about $50 more for a better appliance. [She then added] Of course, you pay $19 for hookup and $10 if we take away your old dryer.

Me: $19 for hookup? Don't I just plug it in?

Clerk: Oh no, the cord is extra. [She then looked at me and I could see the wheels turning.] I suppose your house . . .

Me: Yes [I finished her thought], my house is twenty-five years old.

Clerk: Well, it's no doubt out of code. Does your wall outlet have three prongs and what shape are they? Are they all straight or is one an L shape?

Me: The outlet has three plugs, but I don't know for sure if one is an L.

Clerk: Well, if it's not an L shape, we can't install it. You need an electrician. The warranty is void if you use your old 50 amp outlet. It could start a fire.

Me: I think I'll just use my old electric cord and plug the dryer in until I can get an electrician to change it.

Clerk: [Wrinkling her nose] You would use an old cord? What about dry rot?

Me: [No answer]

Clerk: Now, you should really buy our three-year warranty. It is excellent and adds years to the life of your dryer.

Me: No, thank you.

And I didn't say it, but I wondered if it extended the nine-year average lifetime use and covered dry rot and out-of-code outlets.

I bought the dryer and left Sears. Whatever needed to be changed, we would get changed, but I didn't want this clerk's help doing it. She seemed so smug (pious maybe), telling me how out-of-date I am. I couldn't give her the satisfaction.

That same evening I sat down to enjoy reading my newly arrived copy of *Christianity Today*, a magazine gift from Patty and Mark. Usually this magazine contains thought-provoking articles. But this April issue of *Christianity Today* was different. The controversy! The editorial on the new

TNIV (a new Bible translation) really provoked me. I had all these questions . . .

1. Quick, tell me about the differences in the NIV, RSV, and King James versions of the Bible. Now, the TNIV . . . what is it?

2. Which Bible translation is an ideologically safe alternative for evangelicals? Alternative to what?

3. Are we Lutherans evangelicals?

4. Do you prefer the "dynamic/functional" or "formal equivalence" translations? (This is the thought-for-thought or word-for-word.) This is important.

5. Do you know what an "exegetical eye" is?

Conclusion: I'm out of code. Hopefully I'm "grandfathered in" and won't cause a fire before the Master Electrician comes.

August 22, 2002

Dear Patty,

These are just a lot of thoughts for discussion; I'm not a theologian.

Yesterday we talked about love—how much we loved David, and then our love for Jesus, and it worries us that the depth of our love, by our humanity, doesn't seem correct or poured out where it should be poured out. Do we, can we ever love Jesus as much as we loved David? It doesn't even seem right to think that question, much less ask it. But God, in His infinite wisdom, knows us, and the Bible speaks often to this question. For example, Luke 11:11-13, paraphrased: He asks what man, who is sinful, if his son asks for food, would give a snake? So much more, the Father in heaven loves us and gives to us.

I believe that God blesses us profoundly in the love He lets us experience as a family. He gives us that love so we can glimpse His love. He gave His only Son to die for us so we would know how much He loves us. He knew we could never, of our own accord, being human, understand what His love meant, so He gave His son. That we understand!! If we have loved.

But who can understand God? If we try, we shall fail, and that is what the Bible continually tries to tell us. Our faith is not built on understanding—though we try to do that. We want answers. And I believe we have answers, though not as we would wish.

Why do we think God sent His only Son to die for us, when He could have just appeared in any way He wished? Because we all experience death, the loss of loved ones—it is something we understand. It showed us the depth of God's love when He *gave* his Son for us.

But still we say we loved David more than we love Jesus, or at least that is how we feel. I believe that is okay. It is human love we feel for David. We cannot be like God and know *divine* love, but the depth of the love we feel for David leads us closer to that.

I sometimes think the church does a disservice to the faithful in leading us to think that we can love Jesus (God) as He loves us. It is not possible. Again, the Bible speaks to us as coming like children to the Heavenly Father. A child doesn't really know about love other than what their parents exhibit to them. A child is self-centered—and so are we adults when it comes to God. We loved David for ourselves—for his fun, for all his attributes that we admired. Our love for David is self-centered and loss is very real and painful. But it is not how we should love Jesus. Our love for Jesus should not be self-centered.

So back to the question: Do we love Jesus enough? No. We do not know Divine Love.

For God so loved the world that He gave His only begotten Son, that whosoever *believeth* in Him should not perish but have everlasting life. John 3:16.

It doesn't say whosoever loveth Him, or whosoever understandeth Him—it says whosoever believeth in Him. I have to leave the details to God.

Furthermore, we are grieving the loss of David and feeling very intensely that loss. We are not grieving the loss of Jesus. Imagine how the disciples felt when they lost Jesus. One had betrayed Him and one had denied Him. And now they were on their own—expected to do what Jesus had done! Only when Jesus appears before them again, and they are given the gift of the Holy Spirit, are they able to go on. And these are the ones Jesus chose to be with Him and taught.

David was a gift to us from God—as are all children—and his life and his death have meaning for us. It may take us a long time, but eventually we can be "sorrowful, yet always rejoicing." (II Corinthians 6:10)

We loved David—love means respect, equality, honor—in human terms. We did not worship him. We worship God—we are not on equal terms with God. Therefore, our love of God is fundamentally different.

I think we are worried about something that God would not want us to worry about—in fact, He wants us to trust and obey, not worry.

Love,
Mom

P.S. April 7, 2005. It is the day before the funeral of Pope John Paul II, and people from all faiths saw in him a witness to God's great love. By keeping God's commandment: "This is my commandment, that you love one another, just as I have loved you . . ." (John 15:12), we are expressing our love for God. Our human love, then, becomes divine love.

Bending Light

One of the simplest delights, absolutely free, is watching the patterns cast as rays of sunshine pass through a glass prism. These patterns are the bright, beautiful colors of the rainbow and dance about everywhere as sunlight is refracted. Optimist that I am, I had hung a prism in the entrance hall window to catch the fluctuating and seemingly fickle rays that might come through. January and February seemed to be the best months; the huge trees that surround our home are bare then and the sun is low enough on the horizon to peek in. Occasionally, the "rainbow" danced around the entrance hall.

Karen had also given me an ornament some years ago, a gold angel with six half-inch prisms adorning its skirt, that one could affix to the window by the small suction cup on the back of it. The angel went up high in the corner of the window next to the front door, silent, unobtrusive, just there, seldom reflecting her glory.

Until one morning. I was hurrying through the front hall and happened to glance into the living room, and on the far wall a picture of trees and hills in Colorado, almost monochromic in shades of green, was quite literally undergoing a spectacular transformation. The trees turned shades of red and orange, the mountain in the background shone, and the sky went from gray to blue to an angry storm. The panorama was magnificent. I was incredulous, looking at this picture—suddenly alive—a picture that had been David's!

I glanced around to catch the source of this phenomenon. I knew there was some logical explanation, something rare and instantaneous but logical. Indeed—the rays of sunshine, low in the sky, coming through the entrance hall window were being refracted through the angel's ornamental prisms. These refracted lights, of all colors, were slowly moving across the picture on the opposite wall some thirty feet away, slowly moving as the earth rotated. For a few moments, it seemed, everything was in perfect alignment and I was a witness.

Try as I might, I have never caught that exact moment since.

April 11, 2003

The Touch

There is something I must write down—though to write it down is to put it into human words and I do not have the power to convey in human words God's wondrous presence. Who am I—an insignificant disciple. How dare I say that "He laid His hand upon my shoulder?"

I remember exactly where I was, the conversation I was having with others about how to get my book published, and I made the bold statement, "I will do it. I know this is what God wants me to do." The instant the words were out of my mouth, I felt a hand—a touch—on my shoulder. I sat, stunned, not daring to move, not mentioning it to anyone in the room, wondering what would happen next. Nothing more happened; however, I was affirmed by that touch. That was well over a year ago, and lately I've been thinking that I should write down what I experienced—why, I don't know. I vacillated between wondering if it is arrogance (a spiritual arrogance) on my part to tell this or a false modesty not to tell it.

Then the other day I read again the May 24 devotional in *My Utmost for His Highest*, and Chambers comments on Revelation 1:17. So I went to the Bible to read that part of Revelation ("He laid His right hand upon me"), and it went on in Verse 19 to state, "Write therefore the things you have seen and the things that are . . ."

Lord, forgive me if I am so arrogant, if I believe that one

such as me could be touched by You, the Living God; forgive me if I am so ignorant as to believe You would <u>not</u> come to me.

I struggle. I am in wondrous amazement. I am in anticipation, and yet unsettled. I can identify with Jonah—but of what am I fearful? Of what God will ask of me? I delight in what you, God, teach me, but You know me—undisciplined and impatient. I know that it is blasphemy to think that You cannot, would not, finish a good work that You have begun in me.

So I must be still and know that You are Lord. Psalm 46:10. "Cease striving and know that I am God; I will be exalted among the nations; I will be exalted in the earth."

CHAPTER IV

A WORK IN PROGRESS

For I am confident of this very thing,
that He who began a good work in you
will perfect it until the day of Christ Jesus.
Philippians 1:6

March 23, 2003

"Ownership"

What do I truly own? My house, if it is paid off, but if I don't pay my taxes, it can be taken from me. The same with my car. All of my "possessions" are mine if I continue to take care of them, use them responsibly, and acknowledge that I fit into the larger framework of society. What do I truly own? Unchanging? My own soul and whatever that entails? Am I master of my soul?

Me and mine. How easily we use those words. My children. How I miss "my" David, but he wasn't my possession. He, like all children, was a gift from God. A gift we are given to care for until they can care for themselves . . . a gift we learn from continually . . . a gift we respect as unique souls . . . a gift we delight in (except for those moments when we realize they are uniquely challenging) . . . a gift that, if we don't try to possess, will become independent and reflect God's glory . . . a gift that is freely given and must be freely given up . . . a gift unlike any other.

What do I truly own?

I stood out on the deck at my daughter Patty's home in Colorado one evening and viewed the vast panorama of lights and hills and mountains, and was reflecting on "my" faith. God's gifts of comfort to me when we lost David were extraordinary and had unlocked the key to my soul. But do I have enough faith to withstand inevitable future trials and losses? I felt unsettled. Then I thought, "But I have God and He will see me through."

Instantly the thought was replaced (as though someone interjected the words), "No, God has *you*." I was a little startled—where had that come from? A whisper from without? Within?

A peaceful feeling came over me. I smiled and basked in that new understanding of ownership.

May 2003

"i"

Patty,

Do you remember when we used to sit out on the porch—or on the driveway-in the sunshine and talk about poetry, read poems? Remember ee cummings? He never capitalized "i."

It occurs to me that he was presenting us with a great truth about God, and it becomes more apparent to me daily.

It occurs to me that for at least forty years "I" was more in charge than God—so "I" thought, so "I" acted. Oh, God was always with me—we know that—and He loves us all no matter our arrogance, faults, and sins. He is always trying to break through the big "I."

"I" would say things like, "I will do this with God's help." It was as though God was attached to a tether and brought along with me through life. God wasn't Supreme. But our Lord is so gracious, so humble, so patient—He let me live in that absurdity . . . always trying to teach me in countless ways, and "I" heard and "I" saw His mighty works, but "I" would never really seek deeper understanding.

Over the past forty years, each time I thought I would pursue my own goals, God put a "check" on my plans—illness, or children's needs, or a move overseas, or elderly parents or friends who needed help . . .

I see that now. But over all those years I didn't. I have to admit I thought of myself as someone with a good education, with goals to pursue. Why was I an at-home Mom? What was I ill? Why was I drawn into things I never would have chosen? I was, I might add, thankful I could do some of those things, but they weren't **my** choice.

No, they were God's choices for me. Oh, how blessed I have been. I could never have foreseen what God's "checks" would mean to me.

So what happens to "I"? I know that God loves me and therefore "I" am important as is every other "I" in the human race.

Now He tells me that i am His and all my i's must reflect His will. That does not mean that i am now on His tether—no, He gives me freedom, as He always has, to listen, to wait expectantly for His voice, and to walk His path. He still wants me to be "me" as He created we humans that way, but i now know that pure, unbridled joy comes only through His way, choosing His will.

i now pray that i will always remember to listen, to know that His grace is sufficient for me.

Love,
Mom

CHAPTER V

WE ALL BELONG

. . . so we, who are many, are one body in Christ,
and individually members one of another.
Romans 12:5

You Were Shaped for Serving God

Have Thine Own Way, Lord, Have Thine Own Way; Thou Art the Potter, I Am the Clay.

Isaiah 64:8 - We are the clay - you are the potter.

Several members were asked to give a "temple talk" when our church studied Rick Warren's **The Purpose Driven Life**. *This was my response.*

As God's children, we are shaped for serving Him, for glorifying His holy name. The ways in which we are shaped are as varied as human nature, but perhaps the greatest shaping takes place in the face of the greatest trials. These trials confront us all; it is part of the human condition since the Garden of Eden. Not one of us wants to embrace a trial—no one wants illness or death or loss of a job or divorce or addiction or snipers or terror. But they happen.

Our beloved son, David, was killed on Father's Day 2000 when his Navy demonstration jet crashed at the air show at Willow Grove, PA, and my comfortable, pleasant world crashed too. While I couldn't have expressed it at the time, though, God's grace and love were there with me too. A faith rose in me that I would never have imagined I possessed. My pain was so great that I could not escape it, I could not run from it, I could not hide from it, I could not change it, and so I gave it over completely to God. His grace was there. I did not ask Him if He was going to comfort me, nor how He was going to comfort me. I did not ask, "God, can you help me?" or "God, will you help me?"

No—I called on His promise to comfort me and give me strength. I called on His promise that He would not give me more than I could bear. And His grace was there.

It was there in small ways and extraordinary ways. As someone noted, God's promises, acted on in faith, become prophesy.

Several months after David's accident, around the New Year, I kind of "woke up" one morning and the overpowering thought came to me, "I have to write this down. I have to write about God's gifts of comfort given to me." I looked back in wonder and amazement at the way I had been surrounded, sustained, and carried in an almost incomprehensible way . . . gentle and sweet at the same time.

It is ironic that in times past when I've heard someone witness to God's grace in their lives I was skeptical . . . I thought perhaps they were "overwrought" or exaggerating. Now I stand in front of you and apologize that I do not have the words to adequately describe that time. But I tried to write it down anyway. I wondered if I could look back in years to come and believe it myself. But mostly I knew that I was supposed to write it all down—it was God's commission to me. And at first I thought of what I'd written as a gift for family and friends—to comfort us, to remember David, or for whatever reason God may have had that I did not know. But as time passed, I came to understand that the purpose of my writing, of the gifts of comfort, was to give glory to God for His great love for us, for His incredible resources, which we humans limit by our own thinking; for His gift of faith that sustains us so that, like Paul in II Corinthians 6:10, we can go on "sorrowful yet always rejoicing."

There is a poem in the devotional book *Streams in the Desert* (Cowman 1996), for August 6, that keeps speaking to me, that touches me, that I will share with you . . .

I had a tiny box, a precious box
of human love - my perfume of great price;
I kept it close within my heart of hearts
And scarce would lift the lid lest it should waste
Its fragrance on the air. One day a strange
Deep sorrow came with crushing weight, and fell
Upon my costly treasure, sweet and rare,
And broke the box to pieces. All my heart
Rose in dismay and sorrow at this waste,
But as I mourned, behold a miracle
Of grace divine. My human love was changed
To Heaven's own, and poured in healing streams
On other broken hearts, while soft and clear
A voice above me whispered, "Child of Mine,
With comfort wherewith you were comforted,
From this time forth, go comfort others,
And you will know blest fellowship with Me,
Whose broken heart of love has healed the world."

August 2002

Small Groups

The greatest thing about small groups within the church is who we get to know—God and fellow members through Bible study and fellowship. Sometimes the study is more rigorous and sometimes the social aspect is emphasized, but both are important.

For a long time I didn't connect with the idea that in order to know God, I had to put forth some effort . . . like reading the Bible faithfully and joining in a Bible study.

I also didn't connect with what fellowship and the support of others in the church would mean. Again, in order to know other members, I had to put forth some effort. In our Wisdom Weavers Bible study, we share joys and sorrows, pray for one another, study, laugh, and come to see one another as friends. Some of us are outspoken, others shy; some know their Bible intimately, others of us have to search for each book. We all fit.

Quite spontaneously over time, I have written about two ladies in our group—"Penny's Visit" and "Someone Special." I hope the stories convey something of what my small group means to me.

* * * * * *

"Penny's Visit"

I know this is a story I should tell—my inner voice keeps telling me I should. It isn't a story filled with action, or laughter, or someone speaking great truths. I guess it is a story about silence, about presence, about believers sharing one another's burdens.

I can't give you the exact date or hour or even the length of time involved in my story. That is all lost to me in the fog of emotional despair and exhaustion that followed in the days after we lost our son, David. But the story I want to tell is not forgotten. It is one of the vivid memories of that time that does not leave me.

Penny is a member of the same Bible study that I've attended for a few years. I really don't know her that well in the sense that we haven't spent hours talking about our families, or stories about growing up, or what it is that we truly love to do. She is a businesswoman, quiet, capable, and one senses a strength of character about her.

As I said, I can't remember whether it was one day or five days after we lost David, but one day Penny came to visit, and I was sitting out on the porch in my favorite chair. She sat opposite me in a rocking chair and maybe we visited a little, but I was so exhausted that I think I kept "nodding off." But when I would open my eyes, she was still sitting there just in case I wanted to talk. I remember the reassurance I felt from her presence. She didn't seem uncomfortable about my "lapses"; she didn't seem anxious to be somewhere else, though knowing Penny she probably had many things to do.

Dozens of people had come by to express their sorrow and we so appreciated their visits, but what vividly stays on my mind is Penny's visit—her just "being there." I believe it taught me a lesson: the importance of "being there." As was mentioned in a sermon recently, we overlook the importance of showing up. I know I do. My reasons are numerous. I don't know the people that well, or I don't know what I can say or do that will be helpful, or there will be so many other people there it won't matter if I'm not, or any of the other ad infinitum excuses I have in my "arsenal of self."

That's it. That is my story. As I said, it is not a complex story—just a story about presence, about a visit.

* * * * * *

"Someone Special"

L Love - To know this lady is to love her, this delightful lady whom age graces with 89 years in a way most of us can only hope to attain. I first met her in our Bible study where she listens more than talks, but when she does talk, you appreciate her wisdom. But there is so much more I've learned to appreciate about her.

O Order - You know she's orderly just by visiting her tidy, efficient home, but the order doesn't stop there. She ushers in church, thus assuring that people are comfortable and properly directed for communion. And the order doesn't stop there either. She is a member of various committees in the church. I was chatting with her one day after the service, and a member approached her to remind her of a meeting. I said, "You do that, too?" She just smiled and made a self-effacing remark like "They need someone."

R Resolve - Who else do you know who, when she was told she had breast cancer, said, "Well, I have a trip planned to go to Sweden and I'm going—treatment or no!" I most likely would have retreated into myself, but not her. She proceeded unafraid. That was years ago.

R Recreation - Not a couch potato . . . more on this later. She played tennis until a little health problem stopped her. I play tennis myself, and I think how much I'd like to be on the court with her. Not as her opponent. I have no doubt she'd beat me even if I could play at her level. You see, winning at tennis is at leat 80 percent mental. You have to go out on the court focused and with a determination to win. No, I would want to be her partner on the court. She would keep me focused. So even though she doesn't play tennis anymore, she has that competitive winning edge that keeps her involved and that orderly state of mind that enables her to do it.

A Artist - Her paintings—exhibited in her home—are a delight. But it doesn't stop there. She does needlework (more on that later) and helped design a quilt that the ladies in Day Spring made. I'm told her design capabilities are marvelous. Also, her baked goodies are works of art. If there is going to be a meeting, the best way to assure 100 percent attendance is to announce, in advance, that this lady will be providing the snacks/treats.

I Industrious - My husband, Jim, came home from setting up tables in the church one Wednesday evening a year ago, and he said, "You won't believe who was there helping." Oh yes, I knew, I believed.

N Normal - By now you're beginning to wonder if this person, this lady, is normal. Yes—in spite of the fact that she is a "Norseman," she is normal. In fact, one Sunday last August she did a "normal" thing—she missed a Sunday in church. Yes, there was some excuse like a family reunion in Maryland and a great-great granddaughter, but her absence caused chaos. You see, Jim and I normally sit in a certain row in church that is always anchored on the other end by another regular parishoner, but when this lady was absent that Sunday, we "slipped up" a row, causing great consternation in the regular seating for the Buehlers, Schulstads, Tates, Smiths, and only the Lord knows how many others. All this lady's fault!

E Efficient - This word must surely sound redundant after all I've written, but I have learned that her efficiency has actually given rise to another trait. She has even found time, in the last 30 years, to put her feet up on a footstool—and wear out that footstool! I can imagine she might have even found time to sit and read her Bible!! I discovered all this quite innocently one Sunday recently while chatting with this lady over coffee. She made the remark that she had finally finished a piece of needlework to replace one on a footstool. Not only had she finished the needlework, but she had taken the old piece off and reassembled the footstool. I was impressed! (I have many pieces of needlework lying around waiting to be finished.) Anyway, I asked her what she was going to do with the old piece of needlework she'd taken off and commented that a little wear doesn't ruin a good piece. She immediately responded, "Oh, this is the footstool that I use and I completely wore out the piece." I was astounded! I asked her what

> people would think if they knew how she was using her time. She just laughed! I told her that I wouldn't tell anyone, but then I added, "I may write about it." She just laughed again.

Ha! I may not be able to tell you her name, but I gave 8 big clues!

The Front Door

And I have other sheep, which are not of this fold; I must bring them also, and they shall hear my voice; and they shall become one flock with one shepherd.
John 10:16

The young couple, both "unchurched" and he not baptized, were engaged to be married and wanted a church wedding. A church, its location choice for the participants, had accepted the couple's money, signed a contract, and, if the couple attended the mandatory counseling sessions, would marry them. A date was set, sessions agreed to—months in advance—and then a new minister came to that church. His idea of weddings was not to use them as money raisers for the church and, what's more, the couple was living together. He balked, said he'd "have to think about it," and the couple finally went to the secular domain to speak their wedding vows, thinking that they didn't want to be married by someone who didn't want them.

As I was told this story, I felt the pain of rejection the couple had experienced, and the idea that the church had rejected people whom I love was very grievous to me; then the idea that the church would turn anyone away at the front door became even more grievous to me. So I brought up the subject with a long-time friend who is a Christian and a member of a Bible church, and has studied the Bible extensively. She thought the minister was perfectly correct in objecting to performing the marriage, that churches had to have guidelines and rules and procedures to follow, that the couple could go to a Justice of the Peace and be married—and I don't remember if she used the words "wishy-washy" to describe my attitude, but that is the way I felt about myself after talking with her.

But the thought keeps coming back to me: Didn't the church err? Did the Shepherd lose two of His sheep? And if they weren't His sheep, whose were they?

I do not condone pre-marital living arrangements of any couple, for many reasons—the worldly as well as the spiritual; however, if they were rejected because of their sinful nature, how much more is the church guilty?

For the sin of judgment:

Romans 14:13-23 - Therefore let us not judge one another anymore, but rather determine this—not to put an obstacle or a stumbling block in a brother's way.

Matthew 7:1-5 - Do not judge lest you be judged.

For the sin of hypocrisy:

Romans 3:23 - For all have sinned and fallen short of the Glory of God.

Luke 18:9 - And He also told the parable to certain ones who trusted in themselves that they were righteous and viewed others with contempt.

The questions loom large for me. If we are all sinners (including everyone in the church and we confess that we are every Sunday), how can we reject one another? Because one's sin is more obvious? Do we rank sin? How will the unchurched come to know God if they must be free of sin to enter the front door of the church?

Was the church being taken advantage of because a couple wanted a church wedding? Might they never enter the church again? Perhaps. If that question concerns us, are we more guardians of the church property than of souls?

I realize that these are extremely difficult questions, not only spiritually but in a practical sense. I do not have answers.

I think I am "wishy-washy." I've thought about where I would stand—of what am I absolutely convicted? And it has to be Christ Crucified. But would I be like Peter? Lacking the courage to take a stand?

CHAPTER VI

STEADFAST RENEWAL

Create in me a clean heart, O God,
and renew a right spirit within me.
Psalm 51:10

July 10, 2003

"My God, My God, Why Hast Thou Forsaken Me?"

— Mark 15:34

The question sounds too human, too disbelieving, to be uttered by the Son of God, the Savior of Mankind, and indeed, I've heard it said by more than one person that that question caused them to doubt the entire meaning of the Crucifixion. They ask, "Why did God let His Son suffer so? Why didn't God just take Him into Heaven? Why, if it was God's plan, did Jesus seem to question His death on the cross?" Why? Why? Why?

I've had those same thoughts, but I've come to the understanding that any other statement, or even silence, by Jesus Christ on the cross would have nullified the will of God, would have nullified the prophesies concerning Jesus' death because they would have nullified Jesus' humanity. Jesus came in the form of man to take upon Himself the sins of man, the ultimate result of which is death.

If God had simply taken Jesus into Heaven, as He did Elijah, we humans could not identify with His suffering and death, nor would we have witnesses to His resurrection. Nor would we have understood God's incredible love for us and His courage, nor would we have understood the ultimate sacrifice that was made on our behalf for forgiveness. So Jesus, Beloved Son of God, died a death so undeserving, so untimely, so agonizing, that a shudder goes through our soul. A shudder because in our own moment of agony and/or undeserving and untimely loss, we have asked the very question raised by our Savior: "My God, why have you forsaken me?" Psalm 22:1.

But God, in His omnipotence, had anticipated our human question and so in the ninth hour, as quoted in Mark 15:34 and Matthew 27:46, He had broached it for us first through His Son, Jesus Christ. "My God, my God, why hast thou forsaken me?" His cross has become ours, but we don't understand fully.

Then . . . the question is answered for us, in Mark 15:38. "And the veil of the temple was torn in two from top to bottom." And further in Hebrews 10, verses 19, 20, and 23: "Since therefore, brethren, we have confidence to enter the Holy place by the blood of Jesus, by a new and living way which He inaugurated for us through the veil, that is His flesh . . . . Let us hold fast the confession of our hope without wavering, for He who promised us is faithful."

Personal comment: These thoughts came to mind after reading G. K. Chesterton's book *Orthodoxy* in which Chesterton suggests "doubt" and "temptation" on the part of God in the story of the Passion. His explanation was not made irreverently, but it was emotionally complicated, and I don't believe that God is complicated. In fact, we are asked to become like children in our faith: Matthew 18:3, 19:14.

The Gloxinia and the Hibiscus

While we were living in Norway, a friend had given me a beautiful plant, a gloxinia that in full bloom was incredible in color and form, but of course the flowers withered. I put the plant in a less conspicuous place and wondered if it would ever bloom again. Months passed, and one day as I glanced at the plant, I noticed it had a new flower! I got so excited about that bloom and was so happy that six-year-old David, who was in the room, asked, "Mom, how can you get so excited over a plant blooming?" I was a little embarrassed—why? I can remember throwing out an answer: "If we can't take joy in the little things, what will I be waiting for?" But the child's question and my response never left me.

Now it is April 2001, Good Friday. It has been such a difficult week. I can't stop thinking about David and crying throughout the day as I go about my yard and house work. I'm getting ready for company, but there is no enthusiasm.

I glance at the hibiscus plant that a friend had given me last summer. It is a little plant, only eight inches high, but it had bloomed profusely last summer and fall, beautiful coral-colored blooms. It has been dormant for months now and every time I watered it, and sometimes in between, I kept looking for buds. Today I did the same and saw nothing hopeful as I took it over to the sink to water it. Then, to my delight, as I turned it around to a little bare space to pour in the water, there, at the bottom, almost hidden by the leaves, was a full, beautiful flower. I had been searching at the top of the plant for the flowers but had neglected to look at the bottom, under the leaves, in the part turned to the wall.

Today is June 18, 2001. My hibiscus has not had another bloom since that single, hidden one on Good Friday before Easter.

My response to David some twenty-four years ago had not been complete. At that time, joy was easy to come by. Now I have to look a little harder.

* * * * * *

I've started taking pictures. This story just keeps blossoming—literally! But rather singularly—not like other hibiscus that are full of blooms at one time. This plant has special blooms. Let me tell you about them . . .

There were two blossoms on May 13, the third wedding anniversary of David's lifelong friend. We had driven up to Pennsylvania with David for that wedding, and it was our last time together.

Later—I had been watching a bud for weeks, wondering when it would open (remember the flower only lasts one day)—it began gently unfolding on Father's Day 2003, three years since we lost David.

There were three blossoms on the plant on July 4th and 5th, three years since the funeral for David at Arlington National Cemetery.

It bloomed for the October birthdays, my grandson David and myself, ten days apart.

It bloomed on Thanksgiving.

It bloomed on December 18 when the family arrived from Colorado for Christmas.

It bloomed Christmas Day (I began taking pictures). And the day Patty, Mark, and family left to return to Colorado!

It bloomed on my grandson Darren's birthday.

One day when it bloomed, I couldn't attach any real significance to it—until later that day when there was a knock on the door and it was my friend who had given me the plant! In our phone conversations I had told her about the "bloom schedule" but she had not seen one. I really had to smile. Now I knew why the hibiscus bloomed that day—so my friend could see for herself!

Now, I'm a witness to this cycle of blooms, but I can hardly believe it, or describe the joy I feel at watching a blossom unfold and then, later in the day, the pang I feel as it gently folds back up. No, I don't stand by all day and watch, but it is in my kitchen, by the door, and the blossoms are so incredibly beautiful and intricate; there is nothing slapdash about them. All that for something that only lasts one day—just for our pleasure?

Anyone reading this has probably begun to wonder about me—my far-reaching imagination. I wonder. But consider this: there are 365 days in the year and this plant blooms on significant days. So the cynic might say that in my longing to see God, I could probably find something significant about every day. My response would be, "You are right, but that isn't cynical, you have just given me a Biblical response to God's mystery." — My grace is sufficient for you . . . 2 Corinthians 12:8

Or I could just quote from Oswald Chamber's book *My Utmost For His Highest*:

We look for visions from Heaven, for earthquakes and thunders of God's power . . . . and we never dream that all the time God is in the commonplace things and people around us. (February 7 devotional, p. 38)

Or . . .

> In every wind that blows, in every night and day of the year, in every sign of the sky, in every blossoming and in every weathering of the earth, there is a real coming of God to us if we will simply use our starved imagination to realize it. (February 10 devotional, p. 41)

It is February 25, my husband, Jim's, birthday is tomorrow, and another bloom is about to open—it did!

March 15—a single beautiful bloom. It is our daughter Patty's birthday. Our daughter Karen took a picture with her digital camera to e-mail to Patty. Now Karen says the proof of the "special plant" will be if it blooms on her birthday in June. We all laugh—a little nervously, maybe? No pressure here.

Anger . . . and the "Healing Process"

Another question. This one directed at me.

A lady asked me, a couple of years after we had lost David, how I had dealt with my anger. The question stopped me cold. I didn't know how to respond because one emotion that never raised its ugly head (or healing head?) was anger. I knew that quite often anger is a realistic response to loss, that it is even considered part of the grief healing process. I had wondered if there was something wrong with me for not having anger.

What I did experience was extreme, devastating loss, grief that exhausted me, and anger takes energy that I didn't have. Besides, who would I blame? God for failing to protect our David? What about all the other losses that others experienced?

Should we all be mad at God, this loving God whose purposes we do not comprehend?

Should I be mad at David for choosing such a dangerous profession? Should I be angry with the Navy? How could I be mad when I felt I had to honor his choices?

The one thing that did raise my ire was comments people made about the grief healing process. I remember a remark by a television reporter a few months after 9/11, something about "the families were just getting over the healing process." It seemed to me that those words implied a physical process like healing from an operation or a broken leg.

No, it is not like that. On the other hand, yes, we do have to move forward. But differently. For me, the best analogy I can give to grieving is that it was like a movie playing the story of our lives that was suddenly, inexplicably shut off. How can I start the movie again? Some of it is missing. There is no fast-forward. I push rewind and I go to the beginning, to God, where I started from. Spiritually, I start to toddle but I need support, encouragement, people to teach me. I learn to read and begin to comprehend my faith, what God has given me through his son, Jesus Christ. Then I'm at the teenage/young adult stage—enthusiastic, rather blunt, still asking questions, self-conscious about this process, wanting to tell everyone but not sure how. My words and thoughts are awkward, but I must tell.

When I move into the adult stage (and I pray I do), I will ask for God's continued grace, for wisdom and understanding and continued faith. I found that the Bible truthfully tells us that we can experience sorrow and joy at the same time. I have.

I won't forget David. I don't want to. I do want the "healing process" of God to continue in my life forever.

Shelves

I imagine the shelves in our cluttered basement are not unlike the basement shelves in most other homes. They contain all the items we store from year to year: decorations, sports equipment, boxes with craft items for various hobbies—in other words, all the treasures we'll need at some time or another.

I was in our basement recently looking for all the Christmas decorations, and there wasn't a lot of enthusiasm on my part, as holiday seasons are tinged with an ache of longing. So that was my mood as I moved the ceramic Halloween pumpkin, the box with the Thanksgiving turkey made from sea grass, and the papier-mache Easter bunnies to the back of the shelves and brought forth everything that pertained to Christmas. I no longer use everything but keep it all just in case it can be recycled into some project.

There were also some games on the shelves, and as I rearranged boxes, I saw on top of them a piece of construction paper. I almost ignored it, but curiosity took over and I decided to look before my focus resumed on the task at hand. What was this single piece of paper, folded, I now saw, and out of place on the shelves? What <u>was</u> it?

In child's print on this faded purple folded sheet was David's name with "I love God" written and decorations drawn of flowers, hearts, and stars. At the bottom, also in a child's hand, was written "God's People Long Ago." Inside the folder were lessons about Abraham, Lot, Isaac, Joseph, Moses, Ruth and Naomi, and Samuel.

The lessons were for Grades 1 and 2, which for David was during the time we were living in Norway thirty years ago. (At the time we belonged to the American Lutheran Church in Oslo, a "mission" church connected with the Metropolitan District in the United States.) An entire range of emotions ran through me, but then I wondered how this little "booklet" survived the return from Norway and remained unnoticed all these years. Then the thought came to me of my Bible study lesson for the month and the theme verse: "Keep awake, therefore, for you know neither the day nor the hour." Matthew 25:13. I then also realized how our son, David, had "kept watch," and I'm so thankful for that.

I then began thinking about the great importance of children—and adults too—learning about this great treasure that we have, in all seasons, of God's gift to us of His love. This treasure is not a shelf item to be pulled out for seasonal review, but is one that carries us at all times.

CHAPTER VII

NEAR ENOUGH TO CALL

The Lord is near to all who call upon Him,
To all who call upon Him in truth.
Psalm 145:18

Grace in Conflict

There was something that created conflict between my mother and myself, and as I grew older, if asked, I would say that we loved one another but didn't like one another. Oh, that hurt. I never confided in my mother, or she in me. Even when my first child, Karen, was born and we lived far away, she didn't offer to come, nor did I ask her. Such was our distance, not only in miles but in our hearts.

I wondered about this for years and noted the opposite poles of our personalities. She was practical; I was often impractical. She was not the least philosophical; I was. I loved history and history books; she wasn't interested in the past. I enjoyed baking and fussing over recipes for special meals; she cooked only to have food to eat. I remember a Christmas at our house when my dad and I spent hours preparing Chicken Kiev for seventeen people and my mother was almost angry at our "waste of time." (This was before Price Club, where one can buy prepared, frozen Chicken Kiev.) My mother was a nurse and often made sarcastic remarks about teachers; I wanted to be a teacher!

Was the conflict caused by our differing perceptions of femininity and appearance? What do you do with an undisciplined, self-conscious daughter with red hair and freckles who was a bit of a "tomboy," playing football, baseball, and ice hockey with all the neighborhood kids. I also loved swimming. I bit my fingernails, I was not particularly graceful, and I did not enjoy school—though I did well. All of this must have puzzled my mother, as she was disciplined, graceful, and social (she had wonderful friends). Even when I finished the university and suggested I might want to attend graduate school, I met a resounding "No!" In fact, during the high school years, my parents worried that I wouldn't finish school, and then they worried in college that I would never quit . . . so they told me later. In those days, the ultimate goal for a girl was to marry and have a family.

So the years went. My mother and I were not close and in fact were unkind to one another. On the other hand, I loved my dad and we enjoyed so much the same things, discussing political events, woodworking, and rocks (geology), and though he traveled a great deal, he was the special parent in my life.

Then my dad died suddenly one late August Saturday morning, and now I had just one parent—and not a close one. But I wanted to be close to her, my mother. How? I began to pray for that. Though I didn't understand at the time what prayer meant, I believe Chambers was right when he wrote, "It is not so true that 'prayer changes things' as that prayer changes <u>me</u> and I change things." (Oswald Chambers, *My Utmost for His Highest*, August 28 devotional)

After my father's death, I continued to fly out to Minnesota at least twice a year to visit with her and other family and friends, and we kids supported her desire to sell her home and move into town. My husband, on a business trip to the Midwest, took time to go visit her and to help her find her new home—a perfect, brand-new townhouse where she was content with her wide circle of family and friends and lived for the rest of her life.

But one day she called to tell me that she had had abnormal bleeding and her doctor had scheduled a test to find out the cause. She was now eighty-two years old. I paused and then asked, "Do you want me to come to Minnesota and go with you for your appointment?" Much to my surprise, she said yes. My mother was asking me to be there for her.

And now I began to taste God's grace, His healing touch in my relationship with my mother. I was there when the doctors found my mother's bladder cancer, when the doctor said "maybe another couple of years," then when she went for her checkup every three months—for the next four years. I was there. Sometimes she was clear of any new growths and we celebrated; sometimes another growth would have to be removed and we went through the process. But on all these visits home I began to see my mother as a new "person," and she came to see me as not only a daughter but also a supportive friend. I began to see her sense of humor, her loyalty to friends, her patience with life as it came to her. I joined in playing bridge with her friends, and I attended church with her. We always went to the local Dairy Queen at least once a visit to indulge in a hot fudge sundae. I helped her with house projects and with managing her finances; my brother and sister helped where they could also.

I began to see what it was about me that had contributed to the chasm in our relationship. I could see how things that I had done or ways I had thought puzzled her. She still never confided her deepest feelings or her relationship with God, but she didn't do that with anyone. I had to accept that. But she now regularly told me that she loved me, and I could express that to her also!

As her health deteriorated, I prayed that I could be there when she "fell asleep." I did not want her to be alone. And finally, when a cousin called to say that my mother had had a bad spell, I flew out to Minnesota the next day. That was a Thursday. We had three wonderful days to visit. I washed her hair and set it, and helped her get dressed and come to the table as she wanted to sit and eat meals with me. Friends came to say good-bye. Then on Monday, she slipped into a coma and passed away the following Wednesday. I was with her, holding her hands in mine. Oh, God's abundant grace! He had let me close the wound in my relationship with my mother. There is no way to adequately express what that meant to me.

Illness

I was young then, in my mid-twenties and married with two young children, but I was having some kind of problem with strength in my legs. Numerous doctors gave numerous opinions, and on a summer visit home to my parents in Minnesota, I had an appointment with a specialist at the University of Minnesota—a neurologist with a world reputation as one of the best.

After an examination and conferring with other doctors, he recommended that I enter the hospital for treatment. Until proven otherwise, he said, he thought I had multiple sclerosis. In those days, there weren't too many tests they could run to prove "otherwise." The purpose of the treatments I would receive was to slow or try to stop the progression of the disease, and it meant ten days in the hospital.

My husband, Jim, a naval officer, was at sea, but the Navy gave him leave and he flew to Minnesota to be with me and the children and provide moral support. I was pretty overwhelmed, frightened, and looking to the future with extreme uncertainty. What would happen to me? How would I care for my children, and who would care for them if I couldn't? In my state of mind I envisioned the worst and I let that scenario roll.

The day I was released from the hospital, Jim wanted me to go with him for a brief visit with our long-time friends, Ray and Julie. The visit would be brief because Jim had to leave that evening, but I really didn't want to go—I was afraid to do anything. He gave me a rather blunt pep talk and off we went. While at our friends' house, one of their neighbors stopped in, a lovely, vivacious woman who was expecting her sixth child in a week or so. I looked at her with sheer envy and shrunk further into my self-pity—as I had been told, among other things, that it really wouldn't be wise for me to have any more children. I had two fine daughters and hadn't expressed a desire to have more children, but that didn't matter. I was too caught up in negative thinking.

The children and I returned to our home in Rhode Island, and I was doing fine physically, but the fear of what the future might bring was terrifying and I was almost immobilized. I began praying daily for some kind of peace of mind to help me cope.

One day about six weeks later, a letter from our friend Julie came in the mail, a long letter. It seemed that her neighbor, the vibrant pregnant lady, had died the day after giving birth. Julie was caring for the baby. I read the rest of the letter, but the initial impact of her death was there. I had been envious of that lady, and I felt very small and cowardly at that moment. I also realized that the letter was God's way of answering my prayer. It wasn't that He told me I would never be ill or even that I was healed. He just let me know that I shouldn't live in fear—that we can't predict what will happen, that we shouldn't be envious of others, and that we should take hold of each day and be thankful.

All of that came down on me that day some forty years ago with resounding clarity. I would like to tell you that I've lived perfectly in that understanding since then, but that would assign more strength and courage to me than I possess. I would also like to say that I sought a deeper understanding of God's grace at that time, as there was no question in my mind that God had heard my prayers, but I did not. Like a spoiled child, I just accepted what was given to me and maybe murmured a “thank you.” There was that Great Divide, after all.

But it was an unforgettable lesson about life and God in the midst of life, extending His grace yesterday, today, and tomorrow.

April 2003

A Balloon Story for Holly, My Granddaughter

Dear Holly,

I have a story to tell you, knowing how much you enjoy stories, and this one makes me smile every time I think about it.

But first, a little background to refresh your memory, Holly, because you are part of this story that takes place over a period of time (Valentine's Day to April 9, 2003) and starts in the state of Virginia, continues in Colorado, and ends up back in Virginia!

In February 2003 you, your mom, and your brother, James, were here in Virginia for a vacation. It was February 14, Valentine's Day, and we went to the grocery store for a few items and had only gone a few feet into the store when we noticed all the decorations: balloons, flowers, and plants. Nothing would do but that we had to get some decorations. Difficult choices! The flowers were all admired and finally a dozen roses were selected and a helium-filled balloon—red and purple with big hearts and "I love you" written on it. It also had a trailing decoration to keep it anchored. Delighted with our selections, we finished our shopping and went home to get on with the festivities. Your aunt, uncle, and cousins (the boys) were coming for dinner.

One might have thought that after the Valentine's dinner and party, the balloon might have been deflated or forgotten—except that someone placed that balloon, with its message of "I love you" and decorated all over with hearts, by the trunk in the corner of the living room.

Now, it is important that you know about the history of this trunk, because it stays in the story. The trunk is very special, as it accompanied your Great-Grandma Bergstrom when she left Sweden to come to America. It held everything she owned. There is still the original address label on it for her destination, the little town of Mahtowa in Minnesota—I guess in case the trunk and Great-Grandma got separated. But they stayed together over the years, and finally the trunk came to our house, where it no longer held any treasures . . . but when we lost Uncle Dave, the trunk seemed like just the right place to keep some of his pictures and personal items.

There the balloon stayed, by the trunk, floating high, anchored by the trailing decoration.

So back to our story. You and your family finally returned to Colorado. I say finally, as you were delayed here a few days after one of the biggest snowstorms in the history of snowstorms in Virginia! And in a couple of weeks I followed to stay with you and James in Colorado for a few days while your parents went to a conference. At the end of those five days (we had great weather and much fun), I was at the airport in Denver, sitting on an airplane at the end of the boarding ramp, waiting for the plane's turn to be deiced, when the captain announced that the airport was closing. The worst snowstorm in ninety years started that morning! Of course, we didn't know that when your dad drove me to the airport that morning. I quickly called your folks, and your heroic dad drove back out to the airport to rescue me (6,000 other travelers weren't so lucky). We made it back to your house, barely, as the road closed behind us. So now I would be in Colorado for another six days, as not only three-plus feet of snow intervened but our country went to war with Iraq and air travel and reservations became very difficult.

Wow! So how does all this fit in with my balloon story? I'll get there.

After we got plowed out (one-lane roads), it was very important to your mom that we all go out for dinner with a friend who was also visiting in Colorado—this friend had lost her young son the year before—and so we all met at a restaurant along with other friends for tears, laughter, and remembering. The children were all given balloons and when we left the restaurant, the sister of the little boy who had died wanted to release her balloon to "go to her brother." Then you, Holly, released your balloon "to go to Uncle Dave." And I didn't know it until much later that when you said your prayers that evening with your mom, you prayed "that Uncle Dave would get my balloon."

Finally I returned to Virginia (I told you this was a "back and forth" story) where, to my surprise, the Valentine's Day balloon was still floating high in the air by the trunk. It was March 23rd. I decided on March 27 (Uncle Dave's birthday) that the balloon needed to be set free from its anchor, so I carefully untied it. The balloon didn't move—it now floated in place, ignored, by the trunk in the corner.

One day, however, I was feeling a little lonesome and thinking those kinds of thoughts, and as I turned the corner to go downstairs, there right in front of my face was an "I love you" message—the balloon was coming up the stairs! I smiled. Well, I watched it for a while, wondering where it was heading, when it went into your mother's bedroom (when she was growing up) and there it stayed.

Until today, April 3rd.

I had played tennis for a little while in the morning and was going to change clothes in the bedroom and was first "stretching out" a little. I heard a gentle "thump, thump" and turned to see the balloon coming down the hall into the bedroom. And then I watched in amazement as the "I love you" balloon circled the walls of the bedroom, going slowly right past Uncle Dave's picture and all of the other family pictures, the wedding pictures, and then came back around behind the open closet door, and past Great-Grandma Bergstrom's picture and then dropped down right by the little pictures I have of you, Holly, and James, and over right past a picture of Daniel and Darren. Then it went around the room again and came back and started out of the room and then came back and, dropping down a little, floated right by my face—very slowly—to make sure I got the message!

I had to smile. But I couldn't just stand there and watch this balloon, now headed who knows where, and besides, I had a lot of yard work to do, so off I went into the yard to rake leaves.

When I came back in for lunch, I thought, "I wonder where the balloon went." So I searched and searched. No balloon, not upstairs or downstairs or in the living room or dining room or out on the porch. What?! Now I got serious and, sure enough, found it up in the skylight in the kitchen. Smiled again, I did.

Grandpa and I worked all afternoon in the yard and finally ordered pizza and ate out on the porch picnic table. The porch was a mess because of repair work and painting on the ceiling, but it was a beautiful day. I had to tell the balloon story to Grandpa, which made me wonder if it was still in the skylight . . . No! Now we both searched and searched, all through the house, finally finding the balloon on the porch, on top of a ladder in the corner. Was it there when we ate our pizza? I smiled again.

Now, as I close this story, I will go one last time to see where the balloon has gone. I think it was running out of steam—or at least helium. Back in a minute . . .

Would you believe the balloon is in my closet?! One of the doors was about one-quarter open and peeking out is the balloon. Smiled again.

Love,
Mor Mor

* * * * * *

April 8, 2003

Balloon (Cont.)

This seems to be a story without an end. I thought that when the balloon was now only moving an inch or so above the floor and went into my closet that it would stay there and deflate completely. Not so!

The next morning, Saturday, when I went into the closet for my sweater, the balloon moved out and settled about an inch off the floor in front of the dressing area in our bedroom. There it was when I came home again from tennis, when it moved in front of the mirrors. Now, finally, it occurred to me to take pictures. There was film in the camera and so I clicked away and then went about my activities. When next I noticed (that was about noon or so), the balloon was in front of the grandfather's clock in the entrance hall. Grandpa had bought that grandfather's clock for me after Uncle Dave was born. Finally, in the evening, I began to wonder where the balloon had gone now; it was no longer in the entrance hall. Another quick search, looking around on the floor because by now I didn't think there was enough helium in it to rise.

Incredibly, I finally found the balloon on top of Great Grandma's and David's trunk, almost back where it had started from in the corner of the living room. Neither Grandpa nor I had put it there. Smiled again. More pictures.

But I have a thought. I don't remember which book or author I read that mentioned that God certainly has a special place in His heart for a child's prayer—those innocent, spontaneous, trusting prayers. God answered your prayer, Holly, and while I didn't know it at the time, He answered with my balloon story to you.

CHAPTER VIII

UNDERSTANDING TRUST

Trust in the Lord with all your heart,
and do not lean on your own understanding.
Proverbs 3:5

Pictures/Visions with Purpose

In our society, anyone receiving a "vision" and talking about it is viewed with complete skepticism . . . or worse. At least, that was how I felt about such people. So I sure wasn't going to share my visions/pictures with anyone. Besides, I never called them "visions"—I didn't know what to call these pictures I've been receiving for well over thirty years. I never thought of them in connection with my faith, or lack of it. It never occurred to me. I tried to explain them away with a laugh and a reference to ESP, whatever that is. I had my self-image to think about, and I believed I was of sound mind. Until the last few years, I never even wrote them down.

So I just ignored them as a quirk . . . until we lost our son, David, when his Navy jet crashed. The "vision" I had received (some thirty-one years ago when David was a few days old) was a terrifying picture. I was losing him down a long, white funnel-shaped "something." Was that from God? Was that His way of preparing me for the horrendous loss my family would experience? Was that His way of telling me He was all-knowing and eventually I would have to put my total trust in Him?

I now had questions, and so I asked to meet with one of the ministers of my church. I had to talk about my pictures. I told him that the pictures I received were just that—a picture appears right in front of me, instantaneous and vivid.

There is no sound. The pictures are totally unrelated to what I am doing or even thinking at that moment. They are not a thought. They are not a dream. I have no control over receiving these pictures—I can't conjure them up or prevent them. They are not a premonition. They are a vivid picture and in a flash they are gone, leaving an indelible imprint on the lens of my brain.

The minister offered a wise and simple solution to my confusion over these strange "visions." He told me to pray for whomever or whatever I saw. I should pray that if God wants me to know more or to do something, He will give me insight. Then, after I have prayed, I am not to be concerned. Oh, the simplicity of his advice, the profound simplicity: prayer.

So why write about this now? I have agonized over this for months. I made up a long list of the pros and cons about writing and revealing these "visions." Finally, the pros won out. Maybe those of you who have had similar experiences will be encouraged.

I have written about three of my visions in this chapter—visions hidden in God's mystery. They are like elegant gifts to me that, as I unwrap them, reinforce great treasures of faith: that prayer in all things is essential; that I must trust God; that I am a witness to the living, present, all-powerful God; that our earthly life is transitory; that we believe that which is promised over and over again in the Bible and stated so simply and firmly in John 3:16:

> For God so loved the world that He gave His only begotten Son, that whoever believes in Him should not perish but have eternal life.

> Oh could I tell, ye surely would believe it!
> Oh could I only say what I have seen!
> How should I tell or how can ye receive it;

How, till He bringeth you where I have been?

Oswald Chambers, *My Utmost for His Highest* (New York: Dodd, Mead & Company, 1935, renewed 1963), April 9 devotional

Intercessory Prayer
(based on a "picture")

The summer of 2002 was hot and very dry, and it seemed as though all the plants and trees would just shrivel and die. The heat indexes were at the extremely dangerous code level, and it is against this scenario that I received a "picture," or "vision," on a very hot weekend in late June.

In the "picture" I received there was no movement, no action, no sound . . . all I saw was the lawn area (bordered by the baby pool) and one side of the community center. I clearly saw the window of the lifeguard room at the end of the lawn. On the lawn there was a rectangular hole, perhaps 3' x 2', and the grass curved smoothly around the edges of that hole. I could not see into the hole. While in actuality the lawn there rises steeply up to the driveway, in my "picture" the lawn was flat. That was it. That was my picture—stark, unforgettable, "out of the blue."

So I did what Karen and Pastor Jansen told me I should do when I received a "picture"—pray about it: pray that if there was something God wanted me to do or if someone was in difficulty, that God would give me more information. And then, after I had prayed, not be concerned.

My prayer for safety, therefore, was for all the people involved in activities at the community center—the swim team, dive team, coaches, tennis clinics, and all the children and instructors involved there—especially since the coming week's forecast was for even hotter, dryer days with more dangerous air quality levels. And my grandson, David, was taking tennis lessons.

Now, I'm a member of the community landscape committee, and we had planted several trees and shrubs that spring around the building and grounds. We were now committed to keeping these new plants alive by watering daily, and on Tuesday, June 23, it was my turn to water, which is what I was doing early that morning. I had finished and turned off the water and was putting the hose away when I felt a strange sensation on my legs. I thought I had backed into a juniper shrub and looked down to see bees swarming around my legs, lots of bees.

I quickly ran to the entrance of the building (off the grass), but the bees were all around me, so I ran into the building and down the stairs, thinking I would have to jump into the shower or the pool! But by the time I got down the stairs, the bees seemed gone, and three ladies were there—volunteers clearing out the storage area under the stairs. I felt a little foolish at my quick appearance and told them what had happened. One of the ladies noted there were still two bees circling my head. But those bees quickly left too.

I turned to head back up the stairs to finish my task, but one of the ladies, Eve, a cardiac nurse as it turns out, said, "No, sit down for a few minutes" and she had the lifeguard give me a popsicle. I don't think a minute passed before I felt strange and said, "I need help." Eve caught me as I sank to the floor, and she told one of the other ladies to call 911.

Three rescue vehicles arrived, but not before Eve had started first-aid measures. I do not remember being afraid or even feeling panic. Everyone did what they could and did it efficiently.

On the way to the hospital in the ambulance, though, I began to struggle to breathe, and when the monitors to which I was connected went off, sounding the alarm, the EMT had to give me a shot of adrenalin. In the emergency room I was given more adrenalin when my throat began to swell, I couldn't swallow, and my speech was garbled.

Finally, after a few hours and much medication, I could go home. I now carry an "EpiPen" with me all the time, as I have been warned about even one bee sting and allergic reaction.

But in the emergency room, after things settled down, I had told my daughter Karen about my "picture" and my resulting prayer for the safety of everyone at the community center. And I think about Eve, a cardiac nurse, who just happened to be there on that one morning and knew what to do, who kept me from going back outside where I would have collapsed and no one would have known.

July 2003

A Picture Received

I record here another "picture" received in mid- to late June 2003. As usual, there was no sound or movement associated with the picture, but there were certain understandings. First, the picture:

I saw a figure "floating" in the air, at about the height of fifteen feet above the ground, alongside a medium-sized tree. I say floating because the figure had the body position of someone floating in water. There was no struggle, as body language with arms and legs flailing to regain balance would indicate. Again, there was no movement in the picture. I knew the location of the picture, as I recognized the landscape as that of the side yard at Karen and Jeff's house—though their house was not in the picture. There was a little of the neighbor's house (upper side) in the picture.

That was it. That was the picture—vivid, without further meaning to me except that I seemed to understand the figure was that of a man, not a child or a woman.

So I prayed for the figure, and did not tell Karen. I did not worry about someone falling off a roof or out of the tree because, again, the picture did not convey that meaning to me—the person was not struggling.

Several days later Karen told me that her neighbor, Bob, a young man (thirty-four years old), was not doing well at all. He had struggled valiantly for five years against cancer and had been blinded and paralyzed at times from treatment. Karen and Jeff and other neighbors had helped him and his wife as the struggle with cancer became more intense, but in recent weeks the man was at peace with the idea that he was dying. And indeed, within a few days, he died peacefully at home.

I had met the man only once, briefly, when Karen had taken him to run an errand (just the month before), and I had stayed with the boys at their house. Even that day, the man had shown thoughtfulness—he had insisted that Karen stop at Wendy's on the way home so he could buy "soft drinks" for Karen's boys.

I have come to interpret my "picture" as that of Bob, the young man. Of course, I don't know that for certain. The connection to me was tenuous, but the vision was so powerful that I record it anyway.

I could not help but note that Bob, at thirty-four years of age when he died, was the age our David would have been had he lived. Long life here on earth is not guaranteed no matter one's occupation.

What? What?

What was that? A "vision" given? I saw a car, its left rear side raised up, a concrete barrier nearby. That was it, but it was a small picture, like seeing one quadrant of the TV screen when one tries to view four channels at once. What did it mean? I was somehow associated with the car. Was I going to drive over something with the left rear tire, or back up over something?

Did I really see that picture? It seemed so insignificant and silly at the time that I decided to dismiss it. Why would I get a vision about the left rear side of a car? Forget it.

A few days later my daughter Karen and I were driving together from our homes in Virginia to the Philadelphia airport to meet family members flying in from Colorado. We were all then going to a commemorative ceremony. On my way to pick up Karen at her home, the very strong thought came to me that I should check the tires. I passed by a big sign advertising a national tire company and I thought, "If I have time this morning, I should stop to get the tires checked." Both of our cars are well maintained, and we had only once had a flat tire. Why the sudden worry about the tires? I thought, "I'll check the tires when I get to Karen's." But I didn't—I forgot.

We drove up I-95 and were halfway between Washington and Baltimore when we heard a terrible racket. We blamed the Jeep behind us. Then we looked at each other in alarm as we realized it was us making that noise. We had a flat tire. We were in the left lane of four lanes and couldn't get over to the right in the heavy traffic, so we pulled over on the left. We came to a stop at a bridge area—concrete barriers with no space to get further off the road. We had to back up. We were just off the road—scary!

A highway patrolman came to our rescue, and when he found out we were on our way to meet a flight in Philadelphia and that an hour wait for AAA would make us late, he changed our tire . . . our left rear tire . . . the left rear side of the car was raised up on a jack.

We were quickly on our way again and I had to tell Karen about that vision. I was dismayed and exhilarated at the same time: dismayed that I had dismissed that vision as too insignificant, and exhilarated that God would know even the smallest details of my life.

Now I felt a certainty about why I had that vision. God wants me to trust Him in even the smallest details—a concept I had scorned as well as the people who prayed those prayers about "little" things.

But Jesus says, "Indeed the very hairs of your head are numbered. . . ." Luke 12:7

Had I ever really believed that? My mind couldn't grasp it. Still can't entirely. I did receive His message, though, about trusting Him in all things—a complete, comprehensive, at-all-times-and-in-all-places trust!

CHAPTER IX

SET THE COURSE

Therefore, since we have so great a cloud of witnesses surrounding us . . . let us run with endurance the race that is set before us . . .
Hebrews 12:1

Giving and Receiving

It was a United States savings bond with a face value of $25.00, purchased by my parents fifty years ago, with my name on it as the owner: a gift for my future. In those days there wasn't a lot of extra money and savings went mostly into bonds.

Silently, slowly, the initial $12.50 purchase price of the bond grew, first in my parents' "important papers" metal box, and then in mine. It was ignored, but finally the bond was no longer drawing interest, and I took it to the bank to cash it in—now worth $187.00.

But this money had an added value—sentimental—as both my parents were now gone. It couldn't just go into the checking account for everyday expenses. What to do? An idea took shape.

My parents had been raised in the same small Minnesota town, married there, and their first child was born there, a son who died on his first birthday from strep throat—there was no penicillin then. A terrible loss at an awful time, the midst of the Great Depression.

My folks moved to Montana a few years later and never, ever talked about their first child, our brother Gerald. In fact, we siblings never knew about him until an aunt told us when we were older—seventeen years later. I felt badly for my parents but never really understood what they had endured until we lost our own son. I wish they could have shared their love and loss with my brother, sister, and me.

So I wrote to the minister of the church in that small town in Minnesota, the church in which I had been baptized and that my parents joined when they retired and moved back. I sent the entire amount, explaining that it was in memory of my brother Gerald, and maybe the church nursery needed toys, but it could be used however they wished. I didn't expect to hear any more than perhaps an acknowledgment of their receipt of the check.

But it was the beginning of what is best described in Luke 6:38: "Give and it will be given to you; good measure, pressed down, shaken together, running over, they will pour into your lap. For by your standard of measure it will be measured to you in return."

First, the minister of that church called me and asked if she could read some of my letter at a church service. Months later I received a church bulletin announcing the planned dedication of a "Noah's Ark" in Gerald's memory, to be placed at the door to the nursery. Each baby born "into the church" would have their name put on one of the hand-sewn animals to be placed on the Ark. When the child reached three years of age and no longer attended the nursery, the special animal would be given to the child. In the upper corner of the sky above the Ark were two little angels, one with Gerald's name on it.

The wall hanging was dedicated at a church service, pictures were taken and sent to me, and they also sent a framed, hand-sewn angel with Gerald's name on it. In addition, I received a personal letter from a woman who told me that her parents had also lost a child and never, ever mentioned their loss to anyone.

I never dreamed that a relatively small gift would come back to me in so many ways. The surprise and joy it gave me was worth many times over what was given: that gift freely given.

Book "List"

A friend asked if I would list the books that I've read that were particularly helpful to me, and indeed, I have kept a list of all the ones I have read. I started to go through that list, writing up comments on my favorites, when it occurred to me that what was insightful and relevant to me might not be to others.

Besides, I realized that many of the books I had read and re-read were already mentioned in my first book, *I Know This Is What I'm Supposed To Do*, and in this one.

But the final "coup" to my list-making was the chapter on study in Richard Foster's book *The Celebration of Discipline*. I was a little "puffed up" on the number of books I had read until I came across Foster's classic work. It brought me up short in a positive way, and I'm indebted to him for this broader picture.

Foster's chapter on study revealed some major gaps in my approach. For example, he establishes some groundwork for reading, three steps we have to take. He says we must first read to understand, then to interpret, and finally to evaluate a book. This can all be done in one reading when we know how to study. Needless to say, I was just "whipping" through one book after another. So now I went back to re-read a few. Some wonderful truths came out. For example, I had read and enjoyed A. W. Tozer's *The Pursuit of God*, but not until the <u>third</u> reading did I connect with chapter 10 in a new way! That chapter helped guide my thinking about "The Great Divide."

Then there is Oswald Chambers' book *My Utmost For His Highest*, which was given to me by a friend almost fifteen years ago. I tried to read it then, but it made no sense to me. Up on the shelf it went—until a few years ago. I've read through it numerous times since, and I keep uncovering and digging and finding one profound truth after another. There are still parts of his book, first published in 1935, that I find difficult, and I find myself thinking, "I wonder what he meant in that passage. I sure would have liked to discuss that with Chambers."

That brings up another part about books and study that Foster mentions: discussion and experience.

The opportunity to discuss a book with others is enlightening. Ideas and meanings come out that might never have occurred to me, and maybe in a joint discussion we'll come closer to understanding what the author was really saying.

Then experience. We all appreciate a book that parallels our own life experiences. Certainly books about loss were more meaningful to me after our own tragic loss. Gerald Sittser's discussion of grace in his book *A Grace Disguised* was deeply comforting to me, and his description of his "awake dream" (p. 145) was so significant for me as I had experienced something very similar. In fact, it gave me courage to write in my first book about something that seemed beyond words.

So much for my book list!

Looking back I realize that the way I chose the books I read was simple—I read whatever anyone gave me after we lost David, or whatever I could find on faith on my bookshelf. There was no choosing, no creed to follow. Some books were wonderful, others marginal.

Certain names kept coming up in my reading—names of authors that seem to carry great weight in Christian thinking that I know I want to read. Names like St. Augustine, Thomas a Kempes, more of Martin Luther, Brother Ugolino, and even the more contemporary Dag Hammarskjold. I haven't even scratched the surface. As Foster notes, though, it is easy to be overwhelmed thinking about what we haven't read. But don't be. Just read and enjoy what is probably on your own bookshelf, or a book you hear someone quoting, maybe C. S. Lewis, and it will lead you deeper and deeper into that mystery of faith.

I did go out and buy G. K. Chesterton's *Orthodoxy*. Why was he always quoted? I have to say I couldn't have started with this fascinating and challenging book—it would have been "Greek" to me. After reading *Orthodoxy*, the thought occurred to me, "This would be easier to understand if I had a good background in Christian history." I had none. So the next step was to order the quarterly magazine *Christian History and Biography*, which I thoroughly enjoy and which is leading me even farther into the depths of Christianity.

Now, you're probably asking "And what about the Bible?" It doesn't belong on a list. It stands alone. Read it, absorb it, meditate on it. It is the book that keeps instructing and giving. Discuss it, experience it, and grow in understanding. No other book comes close.

> All scripture is inspired by God and profitable for teaching, for reproof, for correction, for training in righteousness, that the man of God may be adequate, equipped for every good work. 2 Timothy 3:16-17

John Newton (1725-1807)

Out of our Christian history comes a story about John Newton whose remarkable life was featured in the Winter 2004 magazine *Christian History and Biography.* Some may recognize his name as the writer of the words to "Amazing Grace." But he was so much more, turning from a life as a slave trader and careless living to God, to become one of England's most beloved and trusted ministers. And his influence on other leading evangelical "greats" of his time was significant. I so enjoyed reading about this famous man of faith and was quite taken by a quote from him to a friend late in life, a quote that I think I understand:

> Whatever I may doubt on other points, I cannot doubt whether there has been a certain gracious transaction between God and my soul.
> (Chris Armstrong, "The Amazingly Graced Life of John Newton," *Christian History & Biography* 81 (Winter 2004): 17-24)

Now to Him who is able to do exceeding abundantly beyond all that we ask or think, according to the power that works within us, to Him be the glory in the church and in Christ Jesus to all generations for ever and ever. Amen.
Ephesians 3:20-21

APPENDIX

From the Washington Post, *June 20, 2000*

Top Navy Fighter Pilot 'Always Gave of Himself'

David Erick Bergstrom was an all-American kid who loved his family, loved his church and loved his country.

Despite a calm and deferential demeanor, all he ever wanted to do was follow his father's footsteps into the edgy lifestyle of flying fighter jets. Family and friends in his Annandale community say the man simply wanted to defend his nation. He "always gave of himself," said George Phillipps [sic], *a Bergstrom family friend and longtime Annandale neighbor.*

After a boyhood in which he was obsessed with joining the Navy, Bergstrom graduated from the Naval Academy and became a radar intercept officer, taking over the rear seat of the military's supersonic F-14 Tomcat. He flew missions over the Balkans and enforced the no-fly zone in Iraq before he was assigned to an elite training group. Soon he became one of four officers in the Atlantic Fleet to demonstrate the powers of his flying machine to the public.

On Sunday, Lt. Bergstrom and the officer piloting his jet died during an air show outside Philadelphia when their F-14 completed a routine maneuver—flying upside down—and crashed into the woods in front of more than 100,000 spectators. The crash, which is under investigation, killed two of the Navy's top fliers in one of the military's most dangerous professions.

"He loved his job. He admitted that it had inherent danger to it, but it was something he said he had to do," Phillipps said. "He was what the movies depict as the good old American kid. He loved what he was doing."

Bergstrom, 31, a 1987 graduate of W.T. Woodson High School, was known around his neighborhood as a jovial person who often organized neighborhood basketball games and coached community basketball. He attended Virginia Tech for one year before following his dream to Annapolis—something Phillipps said was inevitable.

Bergstrom and Lt. William Joseph Dey, 30, of Hightstown, N.J., were killed when their fighter jet crashed at Willow Grove Naval Air Station in Willow Grove, Pa., while they were performing standard flight tactics and wowing the air show crowd with the speed and versatility of their craft. Military officials said they are unsure what caused the F-14 to veer into the woods, but Willow Grove spokeswoman Sherri Jones said nothing appeared abnormal about their 20-minute flight.

"Everything seemed fine," Jones said, adding that the plane swooped across the base before disappearing into a grove of trees about 100 yards away, narrowing missing two civilian buildings. "Then there was a fireball and a puff of smoke."

Bergstrom and Dey represented half of the Atlantic Fleet's elite F-14 demonstration team, and both had been instructors at Fighter Squadron 101, based at the Oceana Naval Air Station in Virginia Beach. Both had been in the Navy for eight years and had logged more than 1,000 flight hours in the F-14, a standard carrier-based fighter jet.

Military officials said the F-14 is no longer in production and will be replaced in 2002 by a new fighter jet, the Super Hornet, which has a longer flight capability and takes advantage of more advanced technology. The F-14s are popularly associated with the movie "Top Gun."

Cmdr. Roxie Merritt, a spokeswoman for the Naval Air Force, U.S. Atlantic Fleet, in Norfolk, said investigators have been talking to witnesses and analyzing videotapes of the crash but have yet to come up with a preliminary explanation. Merritt said the plane, which costs about $35 million, appeared to flip over on its right wing after an inverted maneuver and then careened into the woods.

"It did go down in a civilian housing area, and we're not sure if the pilots had enough control to avoid the houses," Merritt said. "But it didn't hit a house, and there were no civilian casualties."

Merritt said the crash has sent shock waves through the naval aviation community. But she added that there are no plans to suspend air shows, which the Navy considers valuable recruiting tools and one of the few opportunities the military has to show the public how tax money is spent.

"Fighter pilots know they're in a very dangerous job," Merritt said. "It's something they know comes with the turf."

Bibliography

Armstrong, Chris. "The Amazingly Graced Life of John Newton." *Christian History & Biography* 81 (Winter 2004): 17-24.

Bergstrom, Catherine. *I Know This Is What I'm Supposed To Do*. Fairfax, VA: Xulon Press, 2002.

Chambers, Oswald. *My Utmost for His Highest*. New York: Dodd, Mead & Company, 1935.

Chesterton, G. K. *Orthodoxy*. New York: Image Books/Doubleday, 2001.

Cowman, L. B. *Streams in the Desert*. Edited by James Reimann. Grand Rapids, MI: Zondervan Publishing House, 1996.

Foster, Richard J. *Celebration of Discipline*. San Francisco: Harper & Row, 1988.

Sittser, Gerald L. *A Grace Disguised*. Grand Rapids, MI: Zondervan Publishing House, 1995.

Tozer, A. W. *The Pursuit of God*. Camp Hill, PA: Christian Publications, Inc., 1982.

Printed in the United States
34843LVS00002B/112-120